MAKING WAVES
PAUL TRACHTENBERG
CHERRY VALLEY EDITIONS
1986

Cover design by Faye Kicknosway

Library of Congress Cataloging-in-Publication Data

Trachtenberg, Paul, 1948-
    Making Waves.

        I. Surfing—Poetry.   I. Title.
PS3570.R235M3   1985   811'.54   85-18971
ISBN 0-916156-77-X

Cherry Valley Editions are distributed by:
    Beach and Company, Publishers

LAWNDALE, CALIFORNIA

A reformed New York Jew,
a Mormon Utah Dane assembled me
in this place by the shore.
My first salty breath.

My words then romped
through big open spaces.
The sea and salt of this suburb
dissolved the locusts and pogroms.

THE FREEWAY

It divided the sea town
sacrificing my home.
We U-hauled inland,
leavin' the pillar of salt.

The scent of Anaheim's orange blossoms
deafened the pounding surf.
I was numbed by this schism.
I was numbed by this schism.

THE NEW BOY

The principal scanned
my language skills,
graded me like an egg
in a carton.

I entered, shaky,
stared at ponderously
by those clannish fawns
under the Sequoias.

NAKED

Coach Hamblin guarded my fig leaf.
For weeks, my thing was not seen.
Who cared?
Insane modesty besmirched me.

The wind finally wafted the leaf.
I began to see naked bullies
and wimps of all sizes.
I warmed to this stark reality.

ANNETTE FUNICELLO

The queen B of Bikini Beach
was the Latter Day Califia.
She had the potion
to surf into Frankie Avalon's arms.

Her room was furnished
with sand to sand carpeting,
palm-to-palm walls,
Dick Dale in stereo through-out.

CANTEENS

"Magic is the Night" enraptured
Mike's and Nancy's embraces.
"Locomotion" kept the steam goin'
for Ken and Lucy.

"Judy's Turn to Cry" caught
Chrissie's gloating smile.
All the huffs and whimpers
all the sweet revengers,
all the mismatches and tears,
all gone in a "Puff."

FOURTEEN

Lonely inland lad I was
never knowin' when I'd be
out to sea. The hunger
for salt bleached my hair.

I studied absent-mindedly
caring only for Maverick.
Bussed back home, after books,
my pooch and I lay supine
staring in twilight.

INLAND

A sea dream
was my Eden,
as close as the call
of shrieking gulls.

Those banshees would band,
dive towards me yanking.
My feet were elevated
by their efforts.

THE BEACH BOYS

"Surfin' USA", the craze
of the west coast.
Their songs waved
the Bay of Fundy to the Tasman Sea
foaming a' la mode.

The kids of day, like thirsty nomads,
swam from the desert sea
to the soupy blue.
Idle without wheels,
I swam in envy.

RESTRICTED

I was bound by my zone,
inhaling hard, to grow feathers
like the banshees.
I shrieked and shrieked bootlessly.

Oh gulls! Oh gulls! Rescue me!
Whirl me into an airy vortex
away from this barren sea.

BLEACHED

Other lads like Chris Cox
became towheads.
The Beach Boys sprinkled
their sea-salt inland.

I hadn't the nerve
to peroxide my brown hair.
Those seniors with wheels
and new fiber glass boards,
escaped the inland wavelessness.

JAN & DEAN

Bom-sha-bom, white sneakers
and a nordic look—viking ship
slivered down to a twelve foot board.
Blizzards warm to soup.

"Them boys are concomitant
with the sunny Beach Boys."
Sadly, Jan lost his balance,
not on a board, on wheels—
supine in twilight.

A SURF STORY

Gulls frolicking silently
on a desolate broken board.
Did the birds get drunk
on a boy's despair?

Is the boy sobbing in seclusion?
Are the gulls, vultures in disguise?
Is the candy-striped board telling?

WOODY

Glossy boards embedded like whores
in a wooded Chevy.
Those senior lads endowed
with surfin' wax and bleach.

The Chevy surfed Beach Boulevard.
I strung out by the backyard pool,
spreading lotion on my loins
with the Beach Boys on KFWB.

WHEELS

My sister and I
like Bonnie & Clyde
dashed away in dad's wagon.
Smothered with lotion,
we dove through the sand.

Mobile at sixteen, I imbibed
all the rippling blue.
I transported my lust,
pulling floral suits
off bobbing surf boards.

TANS

Coppertone reeked,
a contrast with baby white buns.
The little girl with doggie-yanks
on every yellow trash can,
along with the real girls,
ubiquitous as the sand.

Skimpily dressed beach boys
balancin' blithely in the blue.

DOHENY BEACH

I camped a week with Michael
and his Mormon family.
His dad brought two fine boards.
I brought my floral baggies,
tempted to walk on water.

The Beach Boys & the Beatles,
like the Hatfields & McCoys,
shot guns of different tunes.
Michael & I got good tans
with white noses.

VIETNAM

Senior coach Byrnes
forwarned us of an apocalypse.
I was vexed by his doom.
No sergeant was to clip my wings.

That summer, I immersed
in sand and salt water.
I vowed never to lose
my bronze & streaks of blond.

HIBISCUS

I avoided war, smelling flowers.
I pressed them, taking plant I.D.
I was enshrouded by floral curtains
for years to come.

Fullerton was also too far inland,
oceans from the real.
Near the college at Hillcrest park,
I piled hibiscus over me.

BOXBOY

I got a job putting eggs
on harder stuff in bags.
A proficient chest-beater,
I coralled carts kinetically.

After the last cattle gathered,
shrieking banshees appeared.
Those wind-swept gulls shouted saltily:
"Let go of that job."

FIFTY-NINE CHEVY

An Impala on my lap,
purchased by the Niagara
sweat of baggin'. I tapped
on its furry dash
and blew its lyre-horn.

I tar-surfed Beach Boulevard
like the seniors.
Wowie! Huntington Beach had bro-
ken the spell of twilight.

SOIL COUNTER

My days of bondage
still had a thread.
One of life's impossibilities
is to breathe without bread.

I labored again in Alcatraz
countin' dirty linen.
I got relief from convalescent sheets,
countin' perfumed smocks.

PETER PAN

Countin' soiled smocks ended,
my wings sprouted again.
Walt invited me into his kingdom
to sweep and bus with Mister Clean.

I swept my way into selling candy
in the Neuschwanstein castle.
I alternated my candy smock
with ballooned sleeves
vending in Walt's New Orleans.

THE MAGIC KINGDOM

The key unlocked
wax pirates with real souls
who pillaged Walt's subterrane.
Kegs & casks, and mechanical alley cats—
fixtures of this Carribean inferno.

The French Quarters filled
with filigrees and fritters.
Mint juleps and a Creole trio
strummed blues, furnished
the Quarter's cobbled roads.
Blue Bayou cafe' complete
with Walt's animated fireflies.
"A swamp town Lady" spirit.

THINKING WAS BANNED

Tweedle Dee & Tweedle Dum
were jesters in this kingdom.
Eclectic themes gushed like geysers.
White fudge was Walt's cologne.
Chocolate encirled children's smiles.

Walt's studio films
melted in all the lands.
Davey Crocketts on keel boats
and deerskin canoes.
Robinson's tree house
was a dominant shade
for the jungle cruise's
electric zebras & hippos.

"Have an apple dearie" echoed
from the skyways of tomorrow
to the Matterhorn of Fantasyland.

TRAINS TRACKING VARIOUS THEMES

Desert miner carts derailed,
avoiding falling rocks
and animated bobcats.
The Circus train, pastel-colored
with carved caricatures of sorts,
rode through miniature lands
enchanted by the minds
of Grimm, Andersen & Mother Goose.

The People Mover hovered
over tomorrowland, viewed
shrunken visitors swallowed
in snowflakes.
Walt's monorail ran over a boy
trying to get free from the outside world.
All the tansporters: capsules, trains,
boats, utopia cars, ragtime firetrucks, etc...
disseminated fairy dust in the Merry kingdom.

WALT'S CONTINUUM

Vistors begged for boredom
to even the score.
Cliches commiserated
with exotic prospects
that lurked in dark corners.

Some tracks reached a precipice;
The Mule Train Pack was shelved
after some visitors kept
sliding off saddles.

FLOWER PASSAGE

Thank God for corns and blisters
Moving on foot was a relief
from elevations.
Tweaks of pain kept images intact.

There were real plants; impatiens, bottlebrushes,
flax on Tom Sawyer's Island,
banana plants & philodendrons
inhabitating Jungleland.
Petunias & marigolds designed
Mickey Mouse's face.
California oaks & varieties of acacias—
the Chumash spirit.

GROOMED FOR THE OCCASION

Topiaries were everywhere,
mainly in fantasyland.
Stiff green giraffes,
elephants, bears & seals
intrigued visitors waiting
to board the Small World.
Only the privets and boxwood
felt mistreated and misshapen.

"AND THE BEAT GOES ON"

Jamborees, dances, characters & bands
adrenalized the land—a passion
of protoplasm and synapses
of eclectic visions.
Piano rolls waved main street
possessing visitors
on horse-driven trollies.

Dill pickles, cider
and Daisy Duck lollipops
excited their esophaguses.
Recyled Goofies, Mad Hatters,
Winnie the Poohs, red popcorn stands,
& Disney's special taffy
stapled the everyday new faces.

WALT'S BACKBONE

The hunt for spilled popcorn,
a must performance in Everyland.
Not a kernel unpreyed upon,
swept into sweepers' traps.
Aztec ritual.

The tired hunters
drowned their weary bodies
in lost virginities
of monorail girls.

MASKS

Donald Duck chid Minnie Mouse
between Frontierland and Adventureland.
Was it an act on or off?

The visitors flashed lenses
on the situation.
The intermezzo & costumes
concealed the wrenching.

ROADS

Pinocchio made hay with the dwarves.
He nosed the bosoms of tour guides.
Dopey varnished his wood into flesh.

Jiminy Cricket's advice?
Or was it entrapment,
devised by the fox & alley cat,
high or low road?

WALT'S PARTIES

I became a Disney character,
palling with Mary Poppins.
The three little pigs
doffed their hot costumes.
We drank beer near the kingdom.

To my innocent dismay,
I found out through Mickey,
Alice has been around,
and so has Snow White.
Oh blue sea come rescue me!

LULAR

I wheeled out my cart with
mountains of delectable sweets.
My ballooned sleeves ironed,
my Walt-brite smile ready
for the visitors of the kingdom.

Who was lurkin' & eyein' me?
T'was Lular, the lavatory matron.
Off hours, she nestled
in my new furnished room.

WALT'S FAIRIES

Rudy, Rudy the ragtime piano player
fancied the boys. I was his faun.
He flitted dust like Tinker Bell.

He dressed in red—humongus berry singin'.
"Life is a Breeze in this Merry Kingdom."
Four Irish smiles (pals of Rudy)
on one medley bike,
entered my dressing room.

TONI

I Peter-panned my way
for two years in Fantasyland,
dreading its demise.

I stuck on a lollipop girl
selling her wares in the palace
(I surfed into Italian Toni's shore).
She was bronze with rosy cheeks,
delicious in her candy pink dress.

PETER PAN SYNDROME

I became a sot
and Toni left me in molasses.
I lost her for she was real.
Never-Neverland kept me pickled.

The gulls flew around
shrieking, "Leave Disneyland."
Through daddy's contacts,
I launched a real job.

FLEW THE COOP

I began countin' again.
This time, hair-spray
other foodless wares.
An Alpha-Beta warehouse
became a new Alcatraz.

On weekends, I flew in my Chevy
to Laguna where the gay boys lay.
Those bronze boys had lower tan lines
than the Huntington Beach Boys.

VIETNAM II

Sam called me to stand in line
to see if I was fit.
Young boys in jockies
conveyed like coke bottles
to be filled with
whatever Sam desired.

I saw Sam's head doctor
and bemused him.
I was a bottle
they didn't need to fill.

FLEW THE COOP II

I left in a queer bliss.
I celebrated, scarfin'
nordic balls at the Smorgie.
I digested euphoria.

My clipped wings grew
once again. My feet,
my hair like Mercury's helmet,
endowed me with six wings.
I flew Sam's factory forever.

FLEW THE COOP III

I thumbed on vodka,
picked-up not caring by whom.
A stranger sucked my booze.
I woke, yearnin' for more.

Oh, the gulls unraveled me!
I anchored in Laguna, escaped
countin' the days in Alcatraz,
shriekin' with delight.

BOB KALE

This wild toad ride is vivid.
From bar to bar: The Farm,
Oil Can Harry's & Outer Limits.
(The names changed, the same reality.)

We tripped on Orange Sunshine,
hangin' on Bob—lichen on willow.
The Adonis had designs
for the arms of Hollywood.

LAGUNA

I flew to Laguna
in my fiery Impala.
I landed by the soupy sea
with those shrieks
serenading me.

I dabbled in dope
and looked into a kaliedoscope.
My muscles kept that summer suspended.

SIR ROBERT

That hen took this "rara avis"
under his wing. Like Toni,
he knew I wasn't ready
to wine with ocean breezes.

He taught me words,
to feel my space.
"Be tactile like Whitman," he said.
I've danced with two Walts.

RIDING ON WORDS

Verses developed
by Sir Robert's prodding.
A fiber glass board emerged,
I surfed inside.

I did take jogs
for glimpses of boy seals
balancin' on their boards.
Torn between inner & outer surf.

LAGUNA CHARACTERS

"A Stitch in Time Saves Nine."
I don't know about this with these two.
They wore the same cloth
colored by I Ching.

They grew a tailor shop
on the foot of Sir Robert's abode.
A corn to behold!

SOW'S EAR

Too much dope
rent the seams of these tailors.
They sewed yoga pants
and adopted me
into their mystic world.

Sir Robert sated with sanity,
seared the corn.
The tailors didn't tarry,
they left without a stitch.

SILK PURSE

They opened a downtown toggery.
A thread of me was theirs
like a crazed trinity.
A mystic wave synchronized
with the sea.

Time darned their hearts,
Sir Robert's rift mended.
My patchwork self was pleased
for each had a piece of me.

ANOTHER LAGUNAN

We broke bread
for Mary Baker Eddy.
We chatted like elves
in his Grimm's Chateau.

After our reverent rendevous,
Kelvin and his collie
slid to Seacliff Park,
seeking other ideas in bushes.

MESSIANIC COMPLEX

Don McMillan was enraptured
by the mystic craze of the day.
With his stylish argot stewin',
allured me into his aura.

We puffed magic cigars
to enhance our plateau.
Heavenly, he was entranced,
makin' me his Mother of God.

LES DECKER

This Libran labored dilingently
keeping his psychedelic toggery tidy.
He had the accoutrements of the day:
tie-dyed dungerees and open-chested muslin shirts
enabling mystics to expose their ankhs.

He yearned to be enveloped
by a desert cloud,
away from this sea blimp.
He sought sheep among yuccas,
his toggery became asphalt.

TEMPLE STREET HOUSE

Twelve Zodiac signs
A smidgen of Rosicrucianism
A pinch of gnosticism
A cupful of Christianity.

They donned their vestures,
lit the frankincense,
chanted Latin and Sanskrit.
A Laguna Utopia.

LAGUNA'S COSMIC BLIMP

Timothy Leary arrested,
allegin' to take us young bloods
out of this hemisphere.
Gurus from the Himalayas
wafted incense to an Oriental beat.

In retrospect, the taste to transcend
was only for that time.
We were earnest to give
Earth's ugly face a lift.

THE URANTIA BOOK

These interchangeable terms
spun me beyond the clouds.
Madame Blavastky could have
written this book.

The whole hierarchy was expounded,
angels with various names
dwelt on different plains.
What a heavenly explanation!

MYSTICISM

Paranhansa Yogananda sprinkled
realization. I watched
for a lotus flower to bloom
on my belly—"Orange Blossom Special."

Eclectic, I strove to be sane,
torn between love & lust,
not knowin' the fine line.
Oh Lotus, rescue me.

GESTALT

I surfed the cosmic wave
indiscriminately.
A coppice of entangled kelp
to be had.

Who was I foolin', climbin' without rungs?
The myriad pieces, I claimed,
were not my concern. "Wipe outs"
were a steady diet indeed.

CLICHE

Ordinary, I was attempting
to take Frost's untrodden way.
Ignite, Cliche Candle!
Allow me that afflatus-leap!

Like Alice, I shrank
with a fervent prayer
into a peculiar realm.
Did I swallow too much salt water?
"Who are you?" asked a big tomato worm.

MYSTIC CRAZE

There was something cozy
about this realm—a poet
in a purple jungle;
creatures hula-hooping
or dancing a passacaglia.

I was on the crest, ready
to kick out, taking a left side.
Grabbin' the rail, I avoided
the curling wave.

SWEPT ASHORE

I surfed into a channel.
Respite. My lungs deflated
from the near "wipe out."
Too many waves shavin' my brain.

Oh gulls! I grabbed their feet
commanded them to fly me
out of this distorted land.
(Undertows are imaginary.)

MOVIN' ON

It's time to make sense
of lust—my uncontrollable alibi.
I packed it, surfed with
Sir Robert to Huntington Beach.

I'm writing
on my fiber glass board,
coming out with odd poems,
building a castle.

NEW SETTLEMENT

This castle engulfed
by peach & pink hibiscus.
This poem is a lei
for Sir Robert's bronze neck.

I flirt about leaping off,
an undulating Whitmanic edge,
knowin' gull wings are waiting.